EVERYTHING HOCKEY

SYDNEY NEWTON

A Crabtree Canopy Book

Crabtree Publishing
crabtreebooks.com

Author
Sydney Newton

Contributors
Jennifer Rivkin
Rachel Stuckey
Jaime Winters

Editors
Sissy McGonagal
Crystal Sikkens

Proofreader
Melissa Boyce

Design
Margaret Salter

Production manager
Candice Campbell

Images
Newscom: p. 54 (top) Paul Hanna/UPI
Wikimedia Commons: p. 5 (top), 6, 8-9, 10, 11 (bottom), 12, 13 (all), 14 (middle), 15, 17 (top right), 18 (all), 19 (all), 21 (bottom left), 22 (all), 23 (all), 24 (all), 25 (top), 26 (all), 27 (all), 28 (all), 29 (all), 30, 31 (top), 32, 33, 34 (all), 35 (all), 36 (all), 37 (all), 38, 39 (all), 40, 41, 42, 43 (all), 44 (all), 45 (top left, bottom left), 46 (all), 47 (top and bottom inset), 48 (bottom), 49 (all), 50 (all), 52 (bottom), 53 (all), 55 (all), 58 (bottom), 59 (all), 60 (all), 61 (all)
Shutterstock.com: p. 4 Jeff Schultes (bottom); 57 Iurii Osadchi (middle); IU Liquid and water photo (bottom); 7 LesPalenik (bottom); 1 ACHPF (middle); 31 meunierd (bottom right); 56 Joaquin Ossorio Castillo (bottom); 5 DarioZg (bottom); 56 Zhukovsky (bottom); 16 Klara_Steffkova (left); 54 fifg (bottom right); 54 kovop (bottom left); 14 meunierd (bottom); front cover Vitalii Vitleo
All other images by Shutterstock.com

Crabtree Publishing

crabtreebooks.com 800-387-7650

In Canada: We acknowledge the financial support of the Government of Canada through the Canada Book Fund for our publishing activities.

Hardcover 978-1-0398-7487-9
Ebook (pdf) 978-1-0398-8177-8
Epub 978-1-0398-8297-3

Published in Canada
Crabtree Publishing
616 Welland Avenue
St. Catharines, Ontario
L2M 5V6

Published in the United States
Crabtree Publishing
347 Fifth Avenue
Suite 1402-145
New York, NY 10016

Library and Archives Canada Cataloguing in Publication
Available at the Library and Archives Canada

Library of Congress Cataloging-in-Publication Data
Available at the Library of Congress

Printed in the U.S.A./CP072026

CONTENTS

INTRODUCTION

HOCKEY WORLD

The puck drops on the ice and players dash for possession. They tear effortlessly across the ice, making incredible dekes**, passes, and shots on goal. Hockey is one of the most fast-paced and exciting games on Earth.**

There are many different hockey leagues. Both men and women play at **professional, amateur,** and **recreational** levels. The National Hockey League (NHL) is the foremost men's professional hockey league in North America. There are other pro and semi-pro hockey leagues in North America, Europe, and Asia as well. NHL players are the top athletes in their sport. Before reaching the NHL, many develop their skills in junior and semi-pro hockey leagues in Canada, the United States, and Europe.

FAST FACT

Hockey is very popular in Canada, Czechia, Finland, Russia, Slovakia, Sweden, and the United States.

Every NHL team is affiliated, or connected, with a team in the American Hockey League (AHL).

Hockey for All

Some countries have men's and women's national teams. They compete in World Championships and the Olympics. The International Ice Hockey Federation (IIHF) organizes international competitions for players of all ages. Many NHL players also play for their native, or home, country's team during these exciting international events.

Pittsburgh Penguins superstar Sidney Crosby has played for Team Canada during international events.

The PWHL

The Professional Women's Hockey League (PWHL) is a North American women's league that began with six teams in the 2023–2024 season. The "original six" teams were Montreal, Ottawa, Toronto, Boston, New York, and Minnesota. Vancouver and Seattle were added in 2025.

CHAPTER 1

THE BIRTH OF HOCKEY

Hockey is a sport with roots in the ancient ball-and-stick games played by different cultures throughout the world.

Ancient Face-Offs

Ancient tablets found in Iraq tell the story of a great warrior king named Gilgamesh who played a hockey-like game called Pukku-Mikku. It was played with a curved stick, or "mikku," and a hollow wooden ring, or "pukku." Ancient Egyptians played a similar game more than 4,000 years ago.

FAST FACT

Bandy is a European winter sport much like hockey. It is played on ice with curved sticks and a ball.

This ancient Greek sculpture shows a hockey-like game that used curved sticks to move a ball.

Hockey's Evolution

The sport that we now call hockey **evolved** over time. In the 1200s, people in Ireland played hurling, a sport which used curved tree branches to hurl a stone or cow droppings into an opponent's goal. Hurling is still a popular sport–although the equipment has changed! In Scotland, a similar game called shinty is still played.

In North America, Indigenous peoples played their own ball-and-stick games, sometimes on ice. Anywhere from 100 to 1,000 men from opposing villages gathered to play ball-and-stick games together.

Hurling teams today play on grass fields called pitches.

When Irish and Scottish newcomers arrived in North America in the 1700s and 1800s, they brought hurling and shinty with them. They began playing these games on frozen ponds and rivers. The games didn't look much like hockey does today though. Teams often had as many as 20 to 30 players each. The puck was often a wooden stopper from a barrel and, when it was shot wide of the goal, it often got lost in a snowbank.

Canadians often call informal games of hockey shinny. The word shinny is believed to have come from the Scottish game of shinty.

Hockey's First Rules

Many places claim to be the "birthplace of hockey" and there is evidence it was first played outdoors on frozen ponds in the early 1800s. The first known indoor hockey game was played at Victoria Skating Rink in Montreal, Quebec, in 1875. Teams had nine players each. Instead of a ball, they used a flat disk-shaped piece of wood. In 1877, the first rules of hockey were published in the Montreal newspaper *The Gazette*. The rules included no forward passing and seven players per team. Goalies were to stay on their feet at all times. Soon, teams everywhere began to follow these rules, and hockey's popularity grew.

The Stanley Factor

In 1883, the Montreal Winter Carnival held the first hockey tournament. The game was a breakaway hit. One fan was Lord Stanley, the Governor General of Canada, who saw his first hockey game at the Montreal Winter Carnival in 1889. Lord Stanley loved it so much that he built an ice rink at his house in Ottawa and started to play the game with sons Arthur and Algernon and daughter Isobel.

People from all over Canada and the U.S. traveled to Quebec for the Montreal Winter Carnival. This winter festival included skating balls, winter sports, and even a giant ice palace made of 10,000 ice blocks!

No boards stood between the ice and the crowd in the Victoria Skating Rink in Montreal, Quebec. The rink was built for skating, not hockey.

The First Stanley Cup

In 1892, Lord Stanley bought a silver bowl and donated it as a prize to be won by the best amateur hockey team in Canada. He paid about $50 for this bowl, which was originally intended to hold punch. He had "**Dominion** Hockey Challenge Cup" engraved on one side, and "From Stanley of Preston" on the other. He entrusted two people to care for and govern, or control, the Challenge Cup. These people came to be known as trustees. Today, the NHL has an agreement with the trustees to take care of the Cup.

The name "Stanley Cup" doesn't appear anywhere on the trophy. It was a nickname given to it and has since become its permanent name.

Playing with the King

Lord Stanley never saw a game played for his Cup. When his brother died in 1893, he and his family had to return to England. However, they brought their love of the game across the ocean with them. In 1895, an extremely cold winter blasted England with snow and ice. The lake at Buckingham Palace froze over and Lord Stanley's sons convinced the Royal Family to play a game of hockey. Lord Stanley and five of his sons hit the ice against six members of the royal court, including the future King George V. Legend has it that the royal court scored once while the Stanley brothers scored so many times that, out of respect, they stopped keeping score. Nevertheless, the Royal Family became fans of the game and watched the Stanley brothers crush several teams outside the palace too.

Lord Stanley

Spreading the Game

Wherever the Stanley brothers played, their skill and enthusiasm increased interest in hockey. By 1903, Europe had a league of five teams. In 1908, the Ligue Internationale de Hockey sur Glace was created for international competitions. Two years later, England won the first European championship. The Ligue later became the International Ice Hockey Federation (IIHF) that governs the sport around the world today.

The International Ice Hockey Federation has 84 member countries. Its headquarters is located in Zurich, Switzerland.

The Challenge Cup

By the late 1800s, many hockey leagues had sprung up across Canada. In 1893, the Montreal Hockey Club became the first winners of Stanley's new Challenge Cup. The only problem was that the winners didn't show up to accept it! The Montreal Hockey Club was arguing with its league about how things were run. Montreal skipped the ceremony in protest. So the league secretly accepted the Cup on their behalf.

The Montreal Hockey Club was formed in 1884.

Early Years

According to the Challenge Cup rules, any league champions could challenge the Cup champion for the Cup at any time during the season. In 1894, Ottawa challenged Montreal. Five thousand fans jammed into Montreal's Victoria Skating Rink for the game. Montreal won 3 to 1. Fans carried the champs out of the rink on their shoulders.

The Montreal Wanderers won four Stanley Cups.

Soon, challengers began lining up to play for the Cup. Since any league champions could call a challenge, the Cup changed hands from league to league, crisscrossing Canada. One year, teams battled for the Stanley Cup four times!

Three Cups

There are actually three Stanley Cups used for different jobs. The original bowl was retired after 71 years, and is on display at the Hockey Hall of Fame. In 1963, a new Presentation Cup was created and in 1993, a replica, or exact copy, of the Presentation Cup was made. This stands at the Hockey Hall of Fame when the Presentation Cup is on the road.

The NHA

John Ambrose O'Brien was a businessman who, with his father M.J. O'Brien, owned the hockey team the Renfrew Creamery Kings. In 1909, the Canadian Hockey Association (CHA) refused to accept his bid to join the league. O'Brien fought back by forming the National Hockey Association (NHA) on the CHA's turf. The NHA made changes to the rules to make the game more exciting. These changes included cutting down the number of players from seven to six, which made games faster and more thrilling. They also changed the number of periods of play from two 30-minute periods to three 20-minute periods. Even with all these exciting changes, the Pacific Coast Hockey Association (PCHA), which formed in 1911, was still able to **lure** talented players to play out west.

In December of 1909, John Ambrose O'Brien founded the Montreal Canadiens and they became part of the NHA. Today, the Canadiens are the oldest professional ice hockey team still operating, and have won the most Stanley Cups of any NHL team.

League Rules

In order to win the Cup, top teams from the eastern and western leagues played best-of-five series. The team that won the most games won the Cup. Since the rules of the game differed between leagues, the rules of the game switched during the series. One game was played by one league's rules and the next game by the other league's rules.

Today, the Stanley Cup spends one day with each of the winning team's players.

Not a Bad Gig

The Stanley Cup is the only professional sports trophy that has a full-time bodyguard. The Keeper of the Cup watches the Cup 24 hours a day, seven days a week. Perhaps that's a good thing. Players have been known to pour milk and cereal in the Cup for breakfast, take the Cup for a dip in a swimming pool, and even drop-kick the Cup like a football. The Keeper of the Cup posts an online travel journal of where the Cup goes. It spends one day with each of the winning team's players in his hometown. Hockey fans can follow the Cup and its adventures as it travels from town to town.

New League

In 1917, bickering team owners tore apart the NHA and formed the National Hockey League (NHL) out of the shreds. The new league competed for players and the Stanley Cup with the PCHA and the Western Canada Hockey League (WCHL) in the prairies.

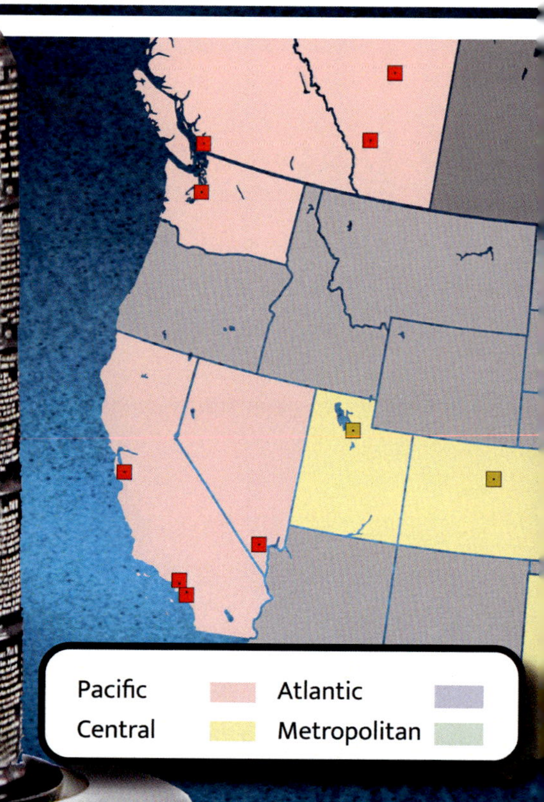

In 1924, the NHL expanded into the U.S. with the addition of the Boston Bruins, and the PCHA and WCHL soon folded, or shut down. By 1926, three more American teams joined the NHL, which was the only league left. Since then, only NHL teams have been allowed to compete for the Stanley Cup.

In 1917, the PCHA team the Seattle Metropolitans became the first U.S. team to win the Cup. They beat the Montreal Canadiens three games to one.

The Conferences

Today, NHL rules determine which teams battle for the Stanley Cup. The NHL divides teams into two groups, called the Eastern **Conference** and the Western Conference. Each conference is split into two divisions. Eight teams from each conference qualify for the playoffs. At the end of the playoffs, the champions from each conference compete in a best-of-seven series to determine the winner of the Stanley Cup.

CHAPTER 2

THE GAME CHANGES

As the NHL evolved, so did the game. Hockey players went from being amateur athletes to pros who were paid top dollar to play the game.

To create a winning team, **scouts**, coaches, and managers look for strong players to fill every position on the ice. Even superstars have to work their way up through the levels of amateur hockey before going pro. Unlike pro athletes, amateurs are not paid to play sports. When hockey first started, all the players were amateurs. They played hockey for the love of it and worked other jobs to make a living.

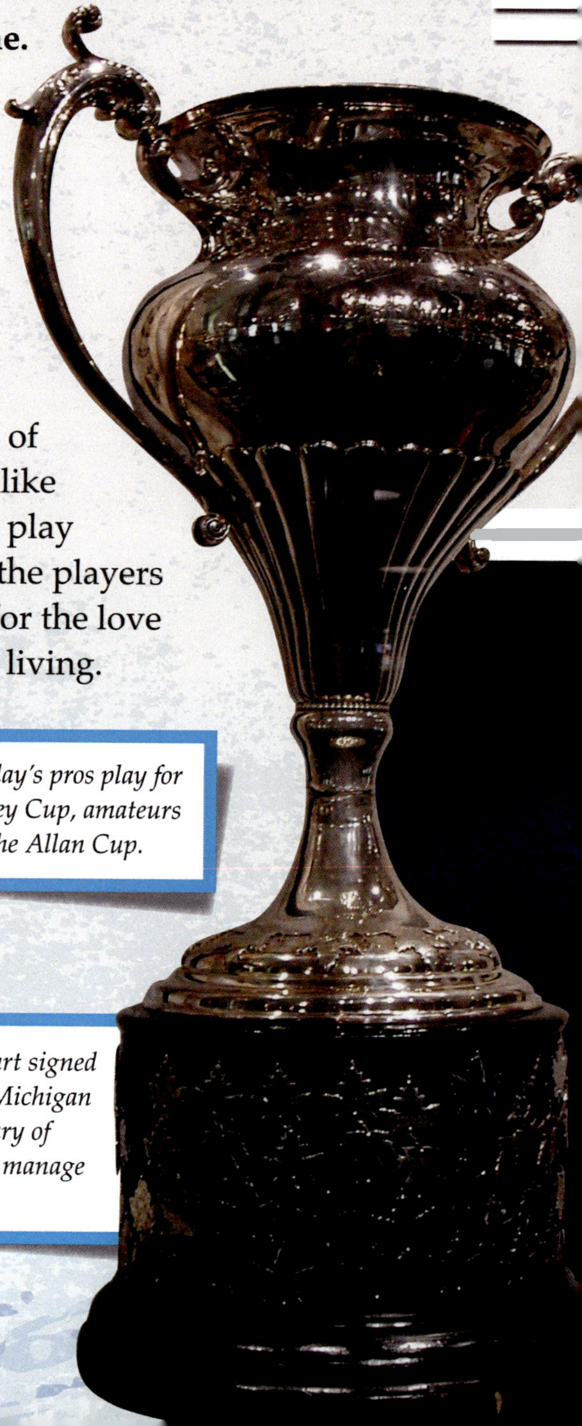

While today's pros play for the Stanley Cup, amateurs play for the Allan Cup.

When defenseman Hod Stuart signed with the first pro league in Michigan in 1903, he negotiated a salary of $1,800 a year to play and to manage the rink.

Going Pro

As team owners **profited** from charging admission to games, and leagues competed for top players who could draw fans to the games, things began to change. Some teams paid players with gifts, such as five-dollar pairs of skates. Others secretly paid them cash and gave them paying day jobs as well. In 1904, the first pro hockey league sprang up in the U.S. It lured Canadian superstars to play for pay—and then there was no stopping hockey from going pro.

Fred "Cyclone" Taylor joined the International Hockey League for more than $3,000 per season.

Banned for Needing Pay

When he was 18, early hockey superstar Fred "Cyclone" Taylor turned down an offer to play for the Toronto Marlboros for lack of money. Playing for the Marlboros would have meant moving from Listowel, Ontario, where he worked in a piano factory doing a job that added $20 a month to his family's income. When he turned down the Toronto Marlboros offer, Taylor was banned from playing anywhere in Ontario. A year later, he left home to play in Manitoba—and became a scoring superstar.

Equipment Changes

As the game changed from amateur to pro, so did the equipment. In the 1800s, hockey players had little in the way of protective gear. Early skates were just a pair of shoes with blades strapped to them. Uniforms were thick wool sweaters. But it wasn't long before players began strapping thick catalogs and books to their shins to shield them from blows from the puck.

Today, players wear crack-resistant plastic shin guards, waterproof padded hockey pants, shoulder pads, padded gloves, groin protectors, mouth guards, and helmets to protect their bodies.

Early hockey sticks were made from carved tree branches. Over time, aluminum, then graphite and ***Kevlar****, were used to make sticks. Today's modern sticks allow players to release quicker and harder shots.*

In the 1920s, players began taping their sticks. The tape improved their grip on the shaft and strengthened the blade. Some players today use black tape on the blade to make it hard for goalies to see the puck on their stick.

Goalie Protection

No player is as grateful as the goalie for the development of protective hockey gear. Early goaltenders did not wear added padding or protective gear. Injuries were common since goalies tried to block shots with their stick, hands, feet, and other body parts. In the 1890s, some began wearing leather goal pads from the game of cricket. As shooters began lifting the puck, goalies borrowed chest protectors from baseball. Once the rules changed to allow goalies to drop to their knees to stop shots, goal pads were developed to protect their knees and keep them dry.

Goalies also invented the blocker and catching glove to protect their hands and help stop shots.

First Mask in Game

In 1959, goalie Jacques Plante took a shot in the face that required 200 stitches. He refused to return to the game without a mask. Jacques Plante became the first NHL goaltender to wear a mask during every game. He developed and tested many different mask designs.

The Original Six

The NHL started with five teams in 1917 and grew to 10 teams. But when the **stock market crash** of 1929 triggered the **Great Depression**, many people fell on hard times. Money and jobs became scarce and several teams folded. By 1943, the NHL had only six teams: the Boston Bruins, Chicago Blackhawks, Detroit Red Wings, Montreal Canadiens, New York Rangers, and Toronto Maple Leafs. These teams became known as the Original Six.

The Great Depression left many people unemployed and unable to afford tickets to events such as NHL games.

The Original Six

Boston Bruins

Chicago Blackhawks

Detroit Red Wings

Fierce Rivals

Over the next 25 years, the Original Six fought tooth and stick for the Cup. Since there were so few teams, the same teams faced each other in the Stanley Cup Finals again and again. Soon, fierce **rivalries** grew between them.

Many teams were stacked with hockey's top players. This led to **dynasties**. These were teams who dominated the game by winning several Cups. The Detroit Red Wings, for example, finished first in the regular season for seven seasons in a row, from 1948–1955. No team has ever been able to do that since.

The Detroit Red Wings were hockey champions in 1952.

Montreal Canadiens

New York Rangers

Toronto Maple Leafs

Building Dynasties

Each dynasty of the Original Six had its own character. In the mid-1940s, the Toronto Maple Leafs rarely finished first in the regular season. They played their best in the playoffs. From 1947–1957, the Detroit Red Wings ruled the league with superstars. In the late 1950s, the Montreal Canadiens were loaded with talented players who practically owned the Cup.

During each season, NHL's best players are selected to be part of the All-Star team. From 1948–1980, Detroit Red Wings superstar Gordie Howe played in 23 All-Star games—the most of any player in the NHL.

Twenty-Four Cups

The Montreal Canadiens (nicknamed "the Habs") are truly part of hockey history. The team was founded in 1909, before the NHL ever existed. Since they joined the league, the Canadiens have won an astounding 24 Stanley Cups. That's more than any other team in the NHL. In fact, the next closest team—the Toronto Maple Leafs—have only 13. The Canadiens have dominated through teamwork, **perseverance**, and the help of superstar players.

Team Rivalry

From 1942–1967, the Cup left the hands of the NHL dynasties only once. And once a dynasty got hold of the Cup, it was tough to break its grip. The Toronto Maple Leafs won the Cup five times in seven seasons. The Red Wings took home the Cup four times in six seasons, while the Canadiens won a record-setting five times in a row. Is it any wonder they were archrivals? When Toronto and Montreal met in the 1951 Stanley Cup Final, they battled so hard that each game of the series went into overtime. Toronto finally emerged with the Cup.

Eric "Sonja" Nesterenko played for the Toronto Maple Leafs from 1951 to 1956 before moving to the Chicago Blackhawks.

Stolen Cup

The Chicago Blackhawks won the Cup in 1961. It was the year after Montreal had set their record with five Cup wins. One Montreal fan was so upset that he stole the Cup out of a display case in the Chicago arena. When a police officer caught him in the act, the fan said, "I want to take it back where it belongs, to Montreal."

Early Superstars

Hockey games were not televised widely until the 1950s—years after hockey legends Gordie Howe and Maurice "The Rocket" Richard joined the NHL. But even though most hockey fans had not seen these two superstars with their own eyes, they had heard about them. Gordie Howe joined the Detroit Red Wings in 1946 when he was just 18 years old. At 6 feet (1.8 m) tall and over 200 pounds (91 kg), he used his size to his advantage. Early in his career, he was known for being a fighter. Later, it was his spectacular hockey skills and energy that people noticed. Howe, who often played right wing, was teamed up with center Sid Abel and left-winger Ted Lindsay to form Detroit's top-scoring forward line, known as "the production line." They placed first, second, and third in the NHL for scoring in 1950.

Ted Lindsay

Sid Abel

Howe went on to become one of the top five scorers in the NHL for 20 straight seasons.

The Rocket

Maurice Richard joined the Montreal Canadiens in 1942 and started out with a bang. He scored five goals in his first 16 games. He led his team to a Stanley Cup victory the following season. He became the league's first player to score 50 goals in a single season. Richard, who was called "The Rocket" because of his speed, was also known for being tough. He was once knocked unconscious during a game and still managed to score the winning goal after he woke up. He also played well under pressure, scoring 82 playoff goals—six of them in overtime.

Maurice Richard

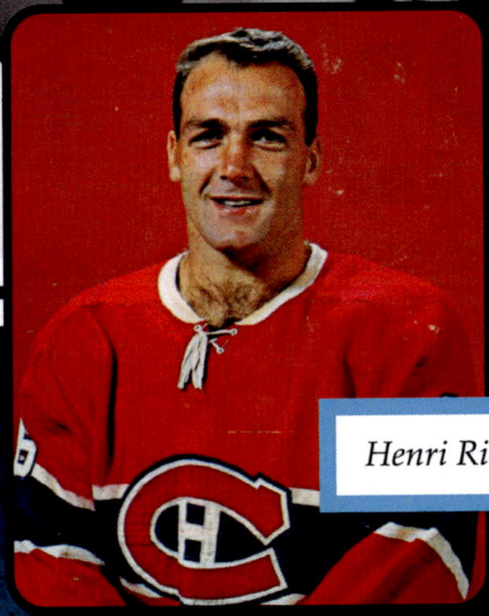

Henri Richard

The Pocket Rocket

Maurice's younger brother Henri also played for the Canadiens (1955–1975). The two were teammates during the later years of Maurice's career. Henri, known as the "pocket rocket," claimed 11 Cup wins—the most in NHL history.

FAST FACT

The NHL named a trophy after The Rocket in 1999. It is awarded to the top goal scorer.

CHAPTER 3

THE EXPANSION ERA

The expansion era is the term used to describe the period of time when the NHL grew in team numbers and markets. Starting with the 1967–1968 NHL season, six new teams were added. By 1974, another six teams were added and the NHL had 21 teams by 1979.

Changes Over Time

The new post-expansion era of the NHL changed the game. The league continued to grow to 32 teams by 2025. Everything from team divisions and conferences to player salaries, number of games played, and season length changed. This fundamentally altered how the game was played.

FAST FACT

The first expansion in 1967 included the Los Angeles Kings, Minnesota North Stars, California Seals (above), Philadelphia Flyers, Pittsburgh Penguins, and St. Louis Blues. This ended the Original Six era.

Los Angeles Kings

Minnesota North Stars

Philadelphia Flyers

Pittsburgh Penguins

St. Louis Blues

A New Pro League

In 1972, the World Hockey Association (WHA) formed. Although the NHL had expanded, the WHA thought more cities would like to have hockey teams. To get top players from the NHL, the WHA offered higher pay. The WHA also challenged a rule, called the reserve clause, that made it difficult for NHL players to leave teams. The rule was changed, and players gained more freedom to switch teams and seek better contracts. In the WHA's first season, 67 players left the NHL for the chance to make more money.

The World Hockey Association had its own trophy known as the Avco World Trophy, or the Avco Cup.

Star in Two Leagues

Bobby Hull was a superstar in both the NHL and the WHA. He won a Stanley Cup with Chicago in 1961. In 1966, he became the first NHL player to score more than 50 goals in a season. However, when the WHA formed in 1972, the average NHL salary was $25,000. Hull became the first to sign with the new WHA, which offered a record-breaking 10-year contract of $2.7 million to the NHL superstar.

Early Winners

In 1974, the Philadelphia Flyers became the first expansion team to win the Cup—and they did it their way. Philadelphia played a very tough, physical game that intimidated other teams. They got into many fights and spent a record number of minutes sitting in the **penalty box**. The Flyers won the Cup again in 1975. But their reign didn't last long. The very next season, Montreal knocked them off Lord Stanley's throne. Even though the games between the two teams were extremely close, Montreal always had the upper hand.

*Dave "The Hammer" Schultz was a top **enforcer** with the Philadelphia Flyers in the 1970s. The first season his team won the Cup, Schultz racked up a record-setting 472 **penalty** minutes.*

Building Anew

The Canadiens' new dynasty was born in the early expansion era. Montreal went on to win four Cups in a row. Along the way, they clashed with Boston. But Boston was no match for Montreal's firepower. In the 1977 Stanley Cup Final, Montreal outscored Boston 16-6, claiming the Cup by winning four games in a row. The next year, they met in the Final again. Boston won two games, but Montreal went on to defeat them again to win the Cup.

Larry Robinson, shown here playing at a post-retirement alumni game, helped Montreal win six straight Stanley Cups in the expansion era. He was ***inducted*** *into the Hockey Hall of Fame in 1995.*

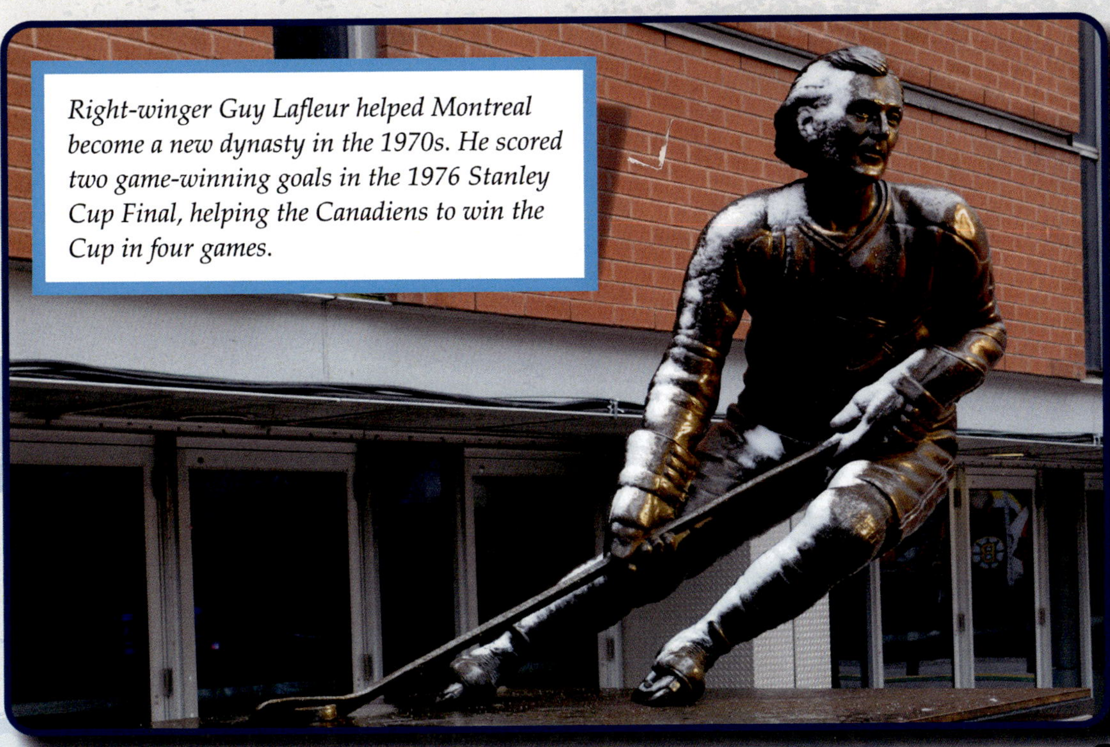

Right-winger Guy Lafleur helped Montreal become a new dynasty in the 1970s. He scored two game-winning goals in the 1976 Stanley Cup Final, helping the Canadiens to win the Cup in four games.

The Great One

In 1979, the WHA folded. Many of its teams and talented young players entered the NHL. This raised the level of play and skill in the league. One of the most talented players the game has ever seen signed with the Edmonton Oilers in 1979. Wayne Gretzky, also known as "The Great One," immediately began shattering record after record. He learned to skate, stickhandle, and shoot on his family's backyard rink in Brantford, Ontario. There, he developed the speed and skill to outplay and outskate players that were much older than him. From 1981, he won seven straight scoring titles. Gretzky was also an amazing passer, with 1,963 assists in his career. Gretzky was traded to the Los Angeles Kings in 1988. He finished his career playing with the New York Rangers. His 894 career goal record stood for 31 years, until broken by Alexander Ovechkin in 2025.

Gretzky set up and scored so many goals that he rewrote the NHL record book.

Islanders Rule

In 1980, the New York Islanders reached the Stanley Cup Final for the first time. They won and became the team to beat, winning the next three Cups too. No U.S. team had won the Cup three times in a row before, let alone four. The fourth time, the Islanders whipped the Edmonton Oilers in four games straight. The Oilers were shocked. Their high-scoring superstars had never scored so few goals. The Islanders had outplayed, outmuscled, and outhustled the Oilers all series long. The Oilers took the lesson to heart. The next year, they beat the Islanders for the Cup. It was the first time an ex-WHA team ever won the Cup. The Oilers won the Cup four more times over the next six years.

Mark Messier was a team leader who won the Stanley Cup six times. Five wins were with the Oilers and one was with the New York Rangers. Messier was also awarded a Conn Smythe Trophy for outstanding player in playoffs, two Hart Trophies for most valuable player, and two Ted Lindsay Awards for outstanding player in a regular season.

CHAPTER 4

HOCKEY SUPERSTARS

The players who become professionals in the NHL are top athletes. Yet even among the pros, there are those who stand above the rest to become hockey legends.

Hockey legends are remembered forever on **memorabilia**, in books and movies, and in the hearts of hockey fans! One such hockey legend was Howie Morenz. In the early days of the NHL, Morenz scored 50 goals per season. From 1923–1937, Morenz played for three teams: the Montreal Canadiens, Chicago Blackhawks, and New York Rangers. He died in 1937 from complications of a broken leg suffered during a game. Morenz was one of the NHL's first superstars in the pre-expansion era. Later superstars played longer seasons but with better equipment to help with the grind.

Brett Hull (above), who played right wing, and his dad Bobby Hull (below), who played left wing, are the only father-son duo in NHL history to each score 1,000 points.

A Family Affair

There have been many fathers, sons, brothers, cousins, and grandsons who have played in the NHL—often against each other. Sometimes family members have played on the same teams. Gordie Howe played on the Houston Aeros and the Hartford Whalers with his sons Mark and Marty.

Nine members of the Sutter family have played, coached, and managed teams in the NHL. Six Sutter brothers from Viking, Alberta, Canada—Brent, Brian, Darryl, Duane, Rich, and Ron—played in the league. All but Rich and Ron also coached and became NHL general managers. Cousins Brandon, Brody, and Brett Sutter also played in the NHL—including a few seasons on the Carolina Hurricanes. Other Sutter cousins were either **drafted** by the NHL or played hockey for other professional leagues.

Phil Esposito is the older brother of fellow Hockey Hall of Famer Tony. The brothers played against each other in the NHL, but with each other on Team Canada in the 1972 Summit Series.

Charlie Conacher (left) played in the NHL from 1929–1941. His brothers Lionel and Roy also played in the NHL, as did his son Pete and his nephews Brian and Murray.

Fantastic Forwards

The best forwards in hockey skate hard toward the **opposition**'s goal, weaving around players who get in their way, to take stunning shots on goal or pass to a teammate who is in a better scoring position. Forwards are aggressive hard workers. While many prefer a specific forward position, most can play right wing, left wing, or center.

Twin-brother teammates Daniel (above) and Henrik Sedin (left) were forwards who played for the Vancouver Canucks their entire NHL careers, from 2000–2018. Daniel became the Canuck's second-highest points scorer—second only to Henrik!

Top 100

Jonathan Toews was the youngest player to become a member of the "**Triple Gold Club**"—he has won an Olympic gold medal, a World Championship gold, and the Stanley Cup. He was named as one of the 100 Greatest NHL Players by the NHL in 2017. Toews played for the Chicago Blackhawks and the Winnipeg Jets. One of the best **face-off** players in the NHL, he won an average of three out of every five face-offs.

Crosby Crushes It

Sidney Crosby is one of the best forwards in the game. His speed helps him avoid defenders. This gives him lots of chances to score. In 2005, at just 18, the Pittsburgh Penguins selected him first in the draft. That year, some people called the draft the "Sidney Crosby Sweepstakes." Adding Crosby to a team was like winning the lottery! Crosby didn't disappoint. The center was named the league's **rookie** of the year after his first season. At 20, he became the youngest player to ever captain an NHL team and was also the league's top scorer and MVP. Two years later, he led the Penguins to a Stanley Cup as the youngest captain to do so in NHL history. It was one of many trophies and awards over the years. In 2017, he was named one of the NHL's 100 greatest players.

Sidney Crosby was the youngest NHL captain to have his name engraved on the Stanley Cup.

Alexander the Great

Alexander Ovechkin is the NHL's all-time leading goal scorer. The left winger earned that title in 2025, when he surpassed Wayne Gretzky's record of 894 goals in 1,487 games. Ovechkin was playing pro hockey in Russia by the time he was 16, but dreamed of playing in the NHL. He signed with the Washington Capitals as the number-one draft pick when he was 17. He scored two goals in the first four minutes of his first game with the Capitals and was named rookie of the year in 2006. Known as a hard-shooting power forward, he has played his entire NHL career with the Caps.

Ovechkin won a Stanley Cup with the Capitals in 2018 and a Conn Smythe Trophy for most valuable player in the playoffs.

Super Mario

Montreal-born Mario Lemieux was named one of the NHL's 100 greatest players despite never playing a full season in his 13-year career due to health problems, including a bout with cancer. The future Hall of Famer started learning to play on his family's frontyard rink when he was just three years old. Drafted in 1984 by the Pittsburgh Penguins, the 6-foot 4-inch (1.9 m) center scored on his first NHL shift. Lemieux helped win two straight Stanley Cups with the Penguins in 1991 and 1992. He also won Olympic gold as captain of the Canadian team in 2002.

When he first retired, Lemieux bought a share of the Penguins. Under his ownership, the Penguins won three Stanley Cups. Lemieux is the only player to have his name on the Cup as both player and owner.

Ageless Wonder

Jaromir Jagr is known for his long playing career. He played for nine NHL teams, winning two Cups and countless other trophies. Jagr has played 38 professional seasons, including his time in both the NHL and Czechia. A right winger, Jagr began skating in his native Czechoslovakia when he was three. By 16, he was one of the best hockey players in the country. He was drafted by the Pittsburgh Penguins at 18, speaking very little English. He was named one of the NHL's 100 greatest players in history.

Jagr's long career and patient playing style earned him the nickname the Ageless Wonder.

A Player's Player

Brad Marchand is a player opposing-team fans love to hate, but one they would all want on their own team. The feisty forward (left wing) played most of his career with the Boston Bruins and gained a reputation as a prickly pest who bugs opponents and steps up to support his fellow players. He's also a top scorer and a four-time NHL All-Star Team pick. Marchand has two Stanley Cups—2011 with the Bruins, and 2025 with the Florida Panthers. In 2024, he was named one of the 100 best Bruins of all time.

Dynamic Defensemen

Defensemen are a goalie's best friends. They sacrifice their bodies to block passes and shots on goal. The best ones can anticipate what the opposition is going to do—and get in their way. They also move the puck out of their zone. Some defensemen, such as Bobby Orr, are also remembered for scoring goals!

Bobby Orr, from Parry Sound, Ontario, was a humble team player—who changed the game of hockey forever. Orr had an amazing ability to defend his zone, earning him eight consecutive Norris Trophies for being the NHL's top defenseman (1968–1976). But unlike most who went before him, Orr also played offensively. He could score! Orr is the only defenseman who was the top scorer in the entire league (yes, including forwards)—twice. At the end of each season, the NHL player who has scored the most goals wins the Art Ross Trophy. Wayne Gretzky won the trophy 10 times in 20 years. Bobby Orr is the only defenseman to win the trophy, and he won it twice!

In the 1970 Stanley Cup Final against the St. Louis Blues, Orr scored the winning goal for the Boston Bruins in overtime. Orr also scored the winning goal in the 1972 Stanley Cup Final.

Big Z

At 6 feet 9 inches (2 m), Slovakian-born Zdeno Chara was the tallest player to have played in the NHL. Nicknamed Big Z for his massive size, Chara moved to North America when he was 19. He played on four NHL teams: the New York Islanders, the Ottawa Senators, the Boston Bruins, and the Washington Capitals. Chara was captain of the Bruins for 14 seasons. He won the Norris Trophy for best defenseman in 2009. That year, the Bruins defense allowed the fewest goals into the net of any team in the NHL. In 2011, Chara helped the Bruins win the Stanley Cup with his intense defensive skills. But his talents also went beyond the defensive zone. Chara had the fastest **slap shot** in the NHL. When he retired in 2022, he held the league's record for all-time games played by a defenseman in the NHL.

The average NHL slap shot is about 87 miles per hour (140 kph). Chara's shots flew at 108.8 miles per hour (175 kph)!

Man Mountain

Shea Weber could be considered one of the NHL's best modern-era defensemen—despite the fact that he never won a Norris Trophy or played on a Cup-winning team. The 6-foot 4-inch (1.9 m), 233-pound (106 kg) defenseman was known for his tough style. Trying to get past Weber was like trying to break through a wall. His shots were extremely fast. Weber played 16 seasons as a Nashville Predator and Montreal Canadien. Like Bobby Orr, Weber had a great all-around game. Like Chara, his shot was one of the hardest in the game. In the 2010 Vancouver Olympics, while playing for his native Canada, Weber's slap shot ripped through the net, straight through to the boards.

Weber's first time playing for Team Canada was at the Vancouver Olympics in 2010. He helped his team capture gold by getting two goals and four assists in seven games.

FAST FACT

Defensemen are also known as blueliners. The name comes from their positioning near the blue line on the ice during offensive plays.

Tough Guy

When he was young, Duncan Keith was told that he would never play in the NHL because he was too small. He proved them wrong. When drafted in 2002, he weighed 152 pounds (69 kg). He trained hard and soon grew to 200 pounds (91 kg) of muscle. Keith was notoriously tough. He lost seven teeth in one 2010 conference final game and kept playing. His claims to fame include two Norris Trophies for top defenseman in the NHL, two Olympic gold medals, three Stanley Cups, and a Conn Smythe Trophy for MVP. He was inducted into the Hockey Hall of Fame in 2025.

Scoring Leader

Ray Bourque played 22 seasons in the NHL. He was a Boston Bruin for 21 years. Bourque holds records for most career goals, assists, and points by a defenseman. He was also team captain longer than any other Bruins player. Bourque played his final year with the Colorado Avalanche. He also played for the Canadian Olympic hockey team. Bourque won the Stanley Cup in his final game in the last season he played!

Great Goalies

Some people say that a team is only as good as its goalie. Goalies don't get to take breaks like other players. They usually stay in net for the whole game. The best goalies can anticipate where the puck is going to go based on its speed and angle, and swiftly block shots with their body, glove, or stick.

Jacques Plante

Jacques Plante was the first NHL goaltender to regularly wear a protective mask. He donned one during a 1959 game when his nose was broken by a shot on net. He left the ice for some stitches and came back with the mask on. Plante's 28-year career (1947–1975) was spent with six teams, most notably the Montreal Canadiens. He won six Stanley Cups with the Canadiens—five of them consecutively.

Glenn Hall

Glenn Hall, nicknamed "Mr. Goalie," was known for his consistency and for rarely missing games. He played for three different teams in the NHL from 1952–1971.

Hall was one of the first to master the butterfly style of goaltending, and won three Vezina Trophies for best goalie.

Gump Worsley

Lorne "Gump" Worsley played for three NHL teams in his 22-year career, refusing to wear a mask until the last six games of his career. Gump won four Stanley Cups in the 1960s and two Vezina Trophies.

Johnny Bower

Nicknamed "The China Wall," Johnny Bower played for two teams in his 24 years in the NHL. He was known for his poke checks, or poking the puck away from opposing players. He won four Stanley Cups in the 1960s and two Vezina Trophies.

Terry Sawchuck

Terry Sawchuck was a rough and tough goalie who played on five NHL teams from 1949–1970. He braved many injuries and received over 400 stitches to his face! Sawchuck held a 30-year record for wins—only matched in 2009. He won four Stanley Cups and was awarded four Vezina Trophies.

butterfly style

Combining Styles

The hybrid style of goaltending is a combination of the older stand-up style and the butterfly style. Most goalies today use a hybrid style. It is more difficult to guess what a goalie is going to do if they use both the butterfly and stand-up styles. Hybrid goalies are very flexible!

hybrid style

Brodeur (above) and his father Denis, who was also a goalie, are the only father-son goaltenders to both win medals at the Olympics. Denis won bronze for Canada in 1956.

Winnipeg Jets goalie Connor Hellebuyck won three Vezinas (2020, 2024, 2025) and a Hart Memorial Trophy for most valuable player (2025).

Marty B

Martin Brodeur was an expert at maneuvering on his skates, getting in position, and chasing down loose pucks. He had many types of saves in his bag of tricks. In addition to being able to butterfly with the best of them, he played well on his feet and had an awesome glove hand. Brodeur had three **shutouts** in his first season with the New Jersey Devils, when he was rookie of the year. He also won three Stanley Cups, two Olympic gold medals, and took home four Vezina Trophies, among other awards. In 2001, Brodeur became the league's all-time leader with 691 career wins. He scored the winning goal on the Canadiens' empty net during the 1997 playoffs.

Saint Patrick

As one of the best goaltenders in the history of the NHL, three-time Vezina winner Patrick Roy played calmly under pressure. This led him to three playoff MVP titles and four Stanley Cups—two with the Montreal Canadiens and two with the Colorado Avalanche. Both teams have retired his number. Roy led the league in shutouts twice in his career and, at the time of his retirement in 2003, he had won more games than any other goaltender in the NHL (551)—later bested by Martin Brodeur. In 2013, Roy went back to the Colorado Avalanche, this time as head coach. He was named the NHL's best coach in 2014, and resigned in 2016.

In January of 2024, Roy returned to coaching, this time as head coach of the New York Islanders.

The Price Is Right

When Carey Price was growing up, the closest indoor rink was a 200-mile (322 km) drive from his hometown in British Columbia. His dad, a former goalie, taught him to play when the creek froze in winter. Later, his dad drove for hours—or flew their four-seater plane—to take Carey to practices. Price played his entire NHL career with the Montreal Canadiens, taking home dozens of trophies, including a Vezina in 2015, and a Masterson for perseverance and sportsmanship in 2022.

CHAPTER 5

OFF-ICE PLAYERS

While hockey's superstar players grab the attention of the fans, some other important "players" in the game are on the side or off the ice entirely. These include league governors and executives, team owners, coaches, trainers, and game officials.

The League

The NHL is the premier professional hockey league in North America and the world. With 32 teams in the United States and Canada, it takes a lot of people to run this big of a show. The league is headquartered in New York City, but teams are located in major centers throughout the two countries.

FAST FACT

The NHL was founded in 1917 with four teams from the original National Hockey Association. Today, there are seven Canadian and 25 American teams.

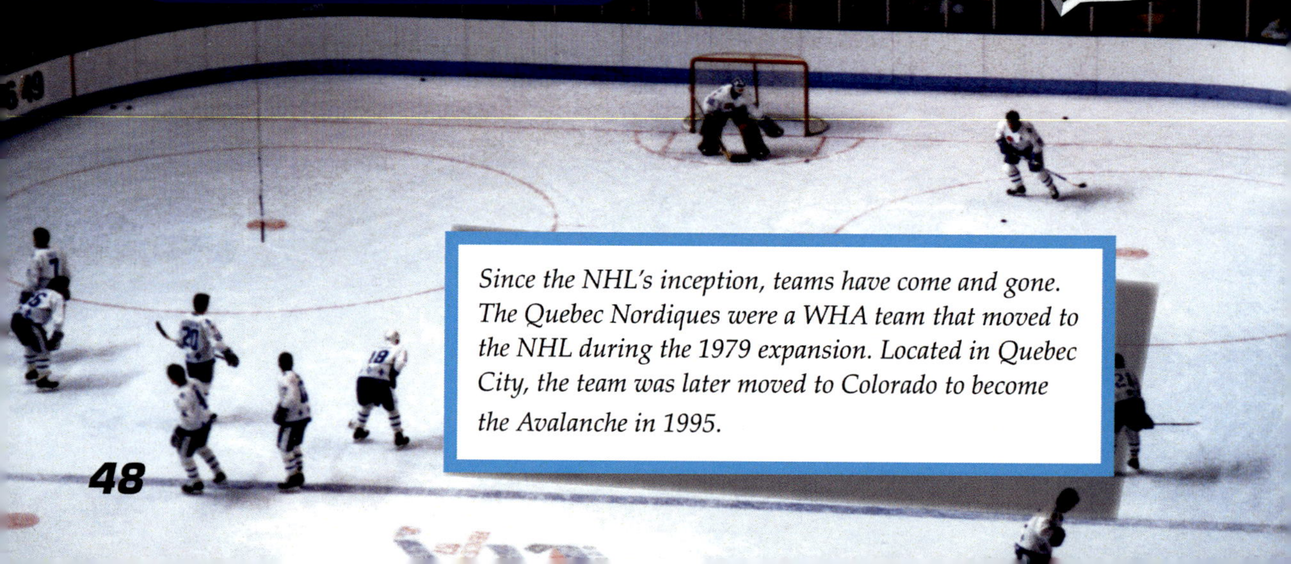

Since the NHL's inception, teams have come and gone. The Quebec Nordiques were a WHA team that moved to the NHL during the 1979 expansion. Located in Quebec City, the team was later moved to Colorado to become the Avalanche in 1995.

Big Boss

The NHL has a Board of Governors which sets league rules. Gary Bettman has been the league's commissioner since 1993. He helped the league expand to 32 teams and made hockey a major sport in new markets, including Nashville, Tennessee (the Predators), Raleigh, Carolina (the Hurricanes), and Dallas, Texas (the Stars). This has increased the growth of hockey as a sport in the United States.

NHL Commissioner Gary Bettman is not always popular with fans, but he brought NHL hockey a greater audience. In 2018, he was inducted into the Hockey Hall of Fame.

Hockey's Champion

Hayley Wickenheiser is one of the most powerful and influential people in professional hockey. Wickenheiser was a powerhouse player who left fans awestruck as one of the most dominating forces in women's hockey. She is an Olympic medal-winning player (four golds, one silver) who made multiple firsts in her 23-year playing career. She's also the first woman assistant general manager of a major NHL team—the Toronto Maple Leafs. While Wickenheiser announced her retirement from playing in 2017, she continues to champion hockey. She also earned a medical degree, something that has helped her understand the physical and mental aspects of professional sports.

Wickenheiser made international history as the first female player to score in a men's professional game while playing in Finland.

Hey Coach!

There are dozens of polls that rank the all-time best NHL coaches. They all list Scotty Bowman as number one. Bowman was head coach of five NHL teams from 1956 to 2002. He won five Cups with the Montreal Canadiens, one with the Pittsburgh Penguins, and three with the Detroit Red Wings. After retirement, he continued working as an advisor and executive with teams that won more Cups, for a record total of 14.

Bowman was inducted into the Hockey Hall of Fame in 1991. He holds the record for most regular season wins in the NHL (1,244) and playoffs (223).

Feisty Owner

Constantine Falkland Cary Smythe, known as Conn, was a feisty owner of the Toronto Maple Leafs (1927–1961) during the team's Cup-winning years. Smythe had served in World War I, and was a prisoner of war with two failed escape attempts. His early nicknames as a coach and owner were "little corporal" and "little dictator." The Conn Smythe Trophy is awarded every year to the NHL's most valuable player in the Stanley Cup playoffs.

NHL Rule Enforcers

The National Hockey League Officials Association (NHLOA) was formed in 1969 to promote and improve the working conditions of the NHL's referees and linespersons. These are the people who are often chirped and not often acknowledged. The Hockey Hall of Fame only started inducting them in 1961.

Cooper Smeaton (1917–1937): Smeaton rejected two offers to play professional hockey in his youth and opted for refereeing instead. He refereed numerous Stanley Cup Finals throughout his career.

Roy "Red" Storey (1950–1959): Storey began his career playing pro football for the Toronto Argonauts. He refereed football, lacrosse, and NHL hockey.

Frank Udvari (1951–1966): Udvari refereed 11 consecutive Stanley Cup Finals. He missed only two NHL games in his entire career—when his wife and father both became very sick. Once, when he was retired, he jumped in on borrowed skates to referee a game after a ref was injured.

Andy Van Hellemond (1972–1996): Van Hellemond was the NHL's top official 14 times. His league records include most regular season games (1,475), most playoff games (227), and most Stanley Cup Finals (19).

Matt Pavelich (1956–1979): Pavelich's brother Marty played for the Detroit Red Wings and the two were often on the ice together. Pavelich was the first NHL linesman inducted into the Hockey Hall of Fame in 1987.

CHAPTER 6

WOMEN'S HOCKEY

FAST FACT

Men and women often played together in just-for-fun games on frozen ponds and rivers where hockey's earliest stars were born.

This is the earliest known photograph of women playing hockey, taken at Rideau Hall, Ottawa, in 1890. Isobel Stanley, Lord Stanley's daughter, is wearing the lighter dress. She was a fan of the game and an influence on her father.

Around 1900, women's hockey leagues popped up in eastern and western Canada and as far north as Dawson City in the Yukon. When men headed for Europe during World War I, women got their first chance to play real hockey.

Leagues of Their Own

Though not everyone thought women should play such a rough-and-tumble game, that didn't stop competitive women's hockey from becoming popular in Canada and the U.S. Both men and women went to games. However, women's hockey didn't receive the same money, equipment, and opportunities that men's hockey did, and it began to lose popularity in the 1940s.

Fanny "Bobbie" Rosenfeld was one of those once-in-a-lifetime athletes who excelled at several sports. She won gold in the 1928 Olympics for the 4 x 100 metres relay and a silver in the 100. She also played hockey and was voted the top women's hockey player in Ontario, Canada, in 1932.

In the 1920s, the Vancouver Amazons played in a tournament with the Seattle Vamps. Some people say this was the first international women's hockey competition.

Eva Ault became a fan favorite playing for the Ottawa Alerts in the early 1900s. She was known as "Queen of the Ice."

League Comeback

In the 1980s, women's hockey made a comeback. More girls and women in North America took up the game than ever before, and a new era of organized women's hockey began.

Until 2021, the top division in women's hockey did not play in the World Championships during an Olympic year. This rule was changed, and in 2022 the Canadian women's team took home gold at the Beijing Winter Olympics in February and then again at the World Championship in September.

The first IIHF Ice Hockey World Championship was held in 1920. The event was for men only. Today, the World Championships are an exciting annual event. Both men and women have the chance to compete, in separate men's and women's tournaments. Since 1977, the World Championships have been open to all players—both amateurs and professionals. Games are played on a larger rink than NHL games. Some rules also differ from NHL rules. For example, in the NHL, players who fight receive penalties. In the World Championships, players who fight are thrown out of the game.

Tournaments

The first IIHF Women's World Championship took place in March 1990 in Ottawa, Canada. Around 85 journalists showed up to cover the action. The players were thrilled with the chance to compete against the best teams in the world. In the Championship Final, Team U.S.A. scored two goals first and Canada roared back with five goals straight to win—setting off a rivalry that continues to this day.

Finland is a top competitor for Canada and the U.S. in both the Women's World Championships and the Olympics. They have won silver once and bronze 15 times in the World Championships. They also have taken home bronze four times in the Olympics.

Another First

In 1992, Manon Rheaume played goalie for the Tampa Bay Lightning in pre-season exhibition games, becoming the first woman to play in a professional men's league.

Olympic Hockey

The Olympic Games take place every four years. In 1988, a rule change allowed professional athletes to compete at the Olympics for the first time. However, it wasn't until 1998 that the NHL changed its schedule to allow its players to play at the Olympics. That was the same year that women's hockey became an Olympic sport. Like the World Championships, the size of the rink and some rules of Olympic hockey vary from the NHL.

In 1998, women's hockey teams got their first chance to compete at the Nagano Olympics in Japan when women's hockey became an official sport of the Games.

Hockey Rivalry

If there is an international competition, such as the Olympics or a World Championship, it is almost certain that the American and Canadian women's hockey teams will meet in the finals. These two teams have always commanded the world of women's hockey, and the rivalry between them is fierce. They have played against each other in all 22 IIHF World Championship Finals except 2019, when Finland took second place against the U.S., leaving Canada with the bronze medal.

In all seven Olympic Games since 1998, Canada and the U.S. have played each other in the finals—except for 2006, when Canada battled Sweden and won gold.

No Body Checking

There is no **body checking** allowed in women's hockey at any level. Some fans believe this is not fair and that women are just as tough as men. But others believe women's hockey is faster and more exciting because there is no body checking. No body checking also means there is less fighting in women's hockey!

Honored Members

The Hockey Hall of Fame started inducting women under the Honored Members category in 2010. Cammi Granato (Team USA) and Angela James (Team Canada) were the first inductees. Only two can be inducted each year, but some years only one, or none, are inducted.

Cammi Granato: Granato was captain of the U.S. women's hockey team that won gold at the 1998 Winter Olympics. She was a 2007 recipient of the Lester Patrick Award that honors hockey players, coaches, or officials who have made significant contributions to ice hockey in the United States. Granato is now an assistant general manager for the NHL's Vancouver Canucks.

Angela James: James is often called the first superstar of modern women's ice hockey. She played for Team Canada in several World Championships, winning four gold medals. James was named the National Women's Hockey League's most valuable player six times, and was one of the first women inducted into the International Ice Hockey Federation Hockey Hall of Fame in 2008. She later moved into coaching and hockey and sports management.

Caroline Ouellette: Ouellette was inducted in 2023. She started playing hockey when she was nine. As a forward, she skated for the Canadian national women's hockey team and the Montreal Stars. She won four Clarkson Cups, four Olympic gold medals, and six World Championships. That makes her one of just a few women to win Triple Gold. Retired from active play, she now coaches Concordia University's women's hockey team.

Riikka Sallinen: Inducted in 2022, Sallinen was born and grew up in Finland where she learned to play hockey with her two older brothers. Sallinen played 16 seasons with Finland's women's national team, winning two Olympic bronze medals, one World Championship silver, and six World Championship bronzes—one of them at age 43.

Jennifer Botterill: A 2025 inductee, Botterill played for Harvard University, the Canadian national women's hockey team, the Mississauga Chiefs, and the Toronto Aeros. She won five World Championships, as well as three golds and one silver at the Winter Olympics. Botterill is now a hockey broadcast television analyst.

Clarkson Cup

The Clarkson Cup was created in 2009 to celebrate excellence in women's hockey. It was viewed as the equivalent to the Stanley Cup and became the ultimate prize in women's hockey. It was awarded to the winner of the Canadian Women's Hockey League (CWHL) championship. Founded in 2007, the CWHL was considered the top women's hockey league in North America until it folded in 2019.

Rival Leagues

A rival league to the Canadian Women's Hockey League formed in March 2015 and ran until June 2023. The National Women's Hockey League (NWHL), later renamed the Premier Hockey Federation (PHF), was a women's professional hockey league that began with four teams and later expanded to seven. The teams, known as the Boston Pride, Buffalo Beauts, Connecticut Whale, Metropolitan Riveters, Minnesota Whitecaps, Montreal Force, and Toronto Six competed for the Lady Isobel Gathorne-Hardy Cup, also known as the Isobel Cup.

Lady Isobel

Pay at Last

The NWHL was the first women's professional hockey league to pay its players. In their first year, each team had a **salary cap** of $270,000 U.S., with each player earning a minimum of $10,000 U.S. In October 2017, the New Jersey Devils signed a three-year partnership with the Metropolitan Riveters. The Devils were the first NHL team to partner with an NWHL team. The partnership gave the Riveters access to facilities for their games and practices and helped them with sponsorship and marketing.

New League

In July 2023, the PHF was dissolved and replaced by the Professional Women's Hockey League (PWHL). The PWHL now has eight teams, with four from Canada (Montreal, Ottawa, Toronto, and Vancouver) and four from the U.S. (New York, Minnesota, Boston, and Seattle). The first-ever game was played between New York and Toronto on January 1, 2024. Initial salaries ranged from $37,000 to $80,000, with a $1.3 million salary cap.

Fans travel from afar to see their favorite PWHL players in action.

GLOSSARY

amateur Someone who does something without pay

body checking In hockey, intentional body contact to try to stop an opponent or take possession of the puck

conference A group of sports teams who compete against one another

dekes Fakes an opponent out of position

Dominion A self-governing country that was part of the British Commonwealth. Canada was a dominion until 1982, when it became fully independent.

draft To choose people, one by one, for sports teams

dynasties Teams that are very powerful or successful for a long period of time

enforcer A hockey player whose main job is to prevent or respond to dirty or violent play by the opposition

evolved Developed over time

face-offs In hockey, how play starts after a penalty or goal

Great Depression A time period during the 1930s when there was worldwide economic hardship. Many people lost their jobs and homes.

hybrid Something that is formed by combining two or more things

inducted Admitted or voted in as a new member

Kevlar A brand of human-made fabric that is very strong and thick

lure To tempt someone to do something, usually by offering some sort of reward

memorabilia (sports) A collection of sports-related objects or materials

opposition The team being played against

penalty Punishment for breaking a rule

penalty box The area off to one side of a hockey rink where players must serve a penalty

perseverance Continued effort to do something, even when it is difficult

professional Someone who is paid for what he or she does

profit To earn or get money from something

recreational Playing for fun

rivalries Competitions between two people or teams to see which ones are the best

rookie A first-year player in a professional sport

salary cap A rule that places a limit on the amount of money that a team can spend on players' salaries

scouts People who evaluate talent

shutouts Games in which one team prevents the opposing team from scoring

slap shot Hitting the puck with the blade of the stick after taking a full backswing

Stock Market Crash In 1929, an event when the value of investments fell rapidly and many people lost their life savings

Triple Gold When three hockey championships, the Stanley or Clarkson Cup, an Olympic gold medal, and the World Championship, are won by the same person

LEARNING MORE

Check out these books and websites to learn more about hockey.

Books

Doeden, Matt. *The Stanley Cup Playoffs: The Quest for Hockey's Biggest Prize.* Millbrook Press, 2020.

Romanuk, Paul. *Hockey Superstars 2025–2026*. Scholastic, 2025.

Smith, Elliott. *Sports Illustrated Kids All-Pro Hockey Almanac.* Capstone Press, 2025.

Zweig, Eric. *The Original Six: Celebrating Hockey's History* series. Crabtree Publishing, 2018.

Websites

www.nhl.com
The NHL website provides information on all the NHL teams and players, along with stats, news, schedules, and more. Click on the players' links to learn all about your favorites!

www.hhof.com
The Hockey Hall of Fame has information on the NHL's biggest dynasties, hockey's historic trophies, and timelines of the Olympics and women's hockey. Visit this website to view photos and learn all about the legends of hockey that have been inducted into the Hall of Fame.

www.olympics.com/en/news/five-things-stanley-cup-ice-hockey-trophy
Learn five interesting facts about the Stanley Cup, hockey's most iconic trophy.

INDEX